MW00438332

Amazing Journeys

Following in
History's Footsteps
by Ian Young

Reading Consultant:
Timothy Rasinski, Ph.D.
Professor of Reading Education
Kent State University

Content Consultant:
Helen Starkweather
Assistant Editor
Smithsonian Magazine

Red Brick™ Learning

Published by Red Brick™ Learning
7825 Telegraph Road, Bloomington, Minnesota 55438
http://www.redbricklearning.com

Copyright © 2004 Red Brick™ Learning. All rights reserved.

Library of Congress Cataloging-in-Publication Data
Young, Ian, 1970–
    Amazing journeys : following in history's footsteps / by Ian Young.
    p. cm.—(High five reading)
    Summary: Introduces the travels and discoveries of some famous explorers
who crossed deserts, sailed seas, scaled mountains, and flew uncharted skies.
    Includes bibliographical references and index.
    ISBN 0-7368-2790-0—ISBN 0-7368-2831-1 (pbk.)
    1. Discoveries in geography—Juvenile literature. 2. Explorers—Juvenile
literature. [1. Discoveries in geography. 2. Explorers.] I. Title. II. Series.
G175.Y68 2003
910.4—dc21
                                    2003009760

Created by Kent Publishing Services, Inc.
Executive Editor: Robbie Butler
Designed by Signature Design Group, Inc.
This publisher has made every effort to trace ownership of all copyrighted
material and to secure necessary permissions. In the event of any questions
arising as to the use of any material, the publisher, while expressing regret for
any inadvertent error, will be happy to make necessary corrections.

Photo Credits:
Cover, pages 22, 25, 26–27, 28, Joel W. Rogers/Corbis; page 4, Doug
Scott/Mountain Camera Picture Library; page 9, David McLain; page 12,
Hulton-Deutsch Collection; page 14, Mountain Camera Archive; page 16,
Captain John Noel/Mountain Camera Picture Library; page 17, Colin
Monteath/Mountain Camera Picture Library; page 18, Galen Rowell/Corbis;
pages 7, 20, 30, 36, 43, Bettmann/Corbis; page 33, Owaki-Kulla/Corbis; page
35, Yankton Daily Press & Dakotan; page 41, Sygma/Corbis

Printed in China.

2 3 4 5 6 08 07 06 05 04

Table of Contents

Repeating History

What was it like to be the first person to sail around the world? Or the first to climb the world's highest mountain? Some people have done more than think about such amazing journeys. Some have followed in the footsteps of the great explorers who made them.

Climber on Mount Everest

Honoring the Explorers

World history contains many tales of epic journeys. We like to read about the great explorers. We like to try and imagine their journeys—what they did and what they saw.

We also honor the courage of these people. There are many ways to do this. We can pass the stories down to our children. We can try and learn more about these explorers. We can even try to repeat what they did!

This book tells the stories of five such amazing journeys. It also tells how each one has been recalled and honored. What journeys do you think you will find here?

---

epic: a type of poem or story about the adventures of great heroes
honor: to show great respect

CHAPTER 1

Marco Polo

Marco Polo traveled far beyond his home in Italy. He visited a mighty empire in the East. Or did he? Even today, people wonder if Polo told the truth about what he saw. Read on and see what you think.

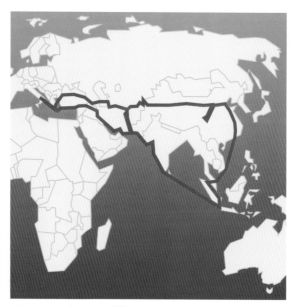

Marco Polo's possible route

Journey to the East

The 13th century was very different from our world today. People in Europe knew little about China and the other countries in Asia. Miles of high mountains and hot deserts lay between them.

In 1271, Marco Polo left Venice, Italy, for China. The young explorer traveled by horse, by cart, and on foot. He crossed Armenia, Iran (called Persia then), Afghanistan, and Pakistan. Finally, he reached China's capital, Beijing. The 5,600-mile (9,012-kilometer) journey took more than three years!

Polo returned to Italy with many tales of magic and wonder. His stories amazed people. But some didn't believe him. They thought that he was lying.

Marco Polo

Even now, some people are not sure. Did Polo really travel all that way?

Quest for the Truth

More than 700 years later, in 1999, a group of people tried to find the truth about Polo's trek. The expedition, called AsiaQuest, followed the route Polo seemed to describe.

Polo had dictated a book about his travels. He called it *Description of the World.* The AsiaQuest team used the book to guide their trip.

Traveling Back in Time

The 10-person team used old travel methods, too. They rode on horses and camels, just as Polo did. But they also used some modern vehicles, such as bicycles and trains. This made the journey shorter than Polo's. But it was still a long way.

The AsiaQuest team also moved more quickly than Polo. They completed their 3,000-mile (4,828-kilometer) journey in just five weeks!

---

trek: a long, slow journey
expedition: a group making a long trip for a special purpose
dictate: to speak aloud while another writes what you say
vehicle: a means of carrying people or things over land

Reporting Home

AsiaQuest kept in touch with schools in the United States during their journey. They wanted children to follow their progress.

AsiaQuest had a computer and a satellite phone. They could connect to the Internet from anywhere on their route. Each day, they sent a report that described what they saw.

What do you think they were looking for on their trip? What do you think they found?

AsiaQuest team members send reports to schools from Dunhuang, China.

satellite: an object put into orbit around a planet or moon

Linking East and West

By the end of their journey, the AsiaQuest team decided Polo had never made it to China. His book does not describe the country as it really was at that time. There are too many facts missing.

The Great Wall of China, for example, is one of the great wonders of the world. Polo would have walked past it in order to reach Beijing. But he doesn't even mention the Great Wall in his writings!

The Great Wall of China

He also does not mention trying Chinese tea or using chopsticks. These are important parts of Chinese life. They were there when Polo made his trip. The AsiaQuest team believes he likely would have written about them if he had really been in China.

Still, Polo played an important role in history. He made Europeans believe that they could go to China. Merchants started to make the journey east. Trade between the East and the West began to flourish. Groups of people met and learned about each other for the first time. The world was never the same again.

Polo traveled many miles to explore China. But not all explorers go looking for new lands. In fact, some can see the end of their journey before they even start. They only need to look up!

---

chopsticks: a pair of small sticks held in one hand and used to lift food to the mouth
European: a person born or living in Europe
merchant: a person who sells goods
flourish: to be successful and prosper

— CHAPTER 2 —

The Everest Mystery

On May 29, 1953, Edmund Hillary and Tenzing Norgay reached the summit of Mount Everest. It was an amazing feat of skill and courage. They were the first to climb the world's highest mountain. Or were they?

Edmund Hillary and Tenzing Norgay

The Challenge of Everest

Mount Everest in the Himalayas (him-ah-LAY-yahs) is the world's tallest mountain. Today, many climbers have scaled it. But less than 100 years ago, no one had reached Everest's summit—an amazing 29,035 feet (8,850 meters) above sea level.

By 1921, no one had climbed higher than 24,600 feet (7,498 meters) on Everest. The air at this height has less oxygen, so it is very hard to breathe. Some people said no one would ever climb to the top.

In 1924, British climbers George Mallory and Andrew Irvine tried to scale Everest. To help them breathe they carried oxygen tanks, much like deep sea divers use.

As Mallory and Irvine neared the top, a bad snowstorm rolled in. What happened next, no one knows. But the two men never came back down.

---

scale: to climb up something; to reach the highest point of
summit: the highest point
oxygen: a gas that all plants and animals need to live

George Mallory and Edward Norton made it to 27,000 feet (8,230 meters) on Everest in a climb on May 21, 1922.

First to the Top?

In 1975, a Chinese climber said he found Irvine's body at 27,000 feet (8,230 meters). The climber died on Everest before he could show anyone else where the body was.

Did Irvine and Mallory reach the top, then fall on the way down? Or did they fall on the way up? Did they reach Everest's summit 30 years before Hillary and Norgay? In April 1999, a U.S. search team, led by Eric Simonson, set out to solve the mystery by following Mallory and Irvine's route.

The Missing Camera

Mallory had taken a pocket-sized camera with him on his journey. If found, the frozen film in the camera could still be developed. It might contain a picture of Mallory and Irvine on the summit. But first, the search team had to find Mallory's body.

A Body is Found

The search team found the decayed body of a fallen climber on May 4. The body was hard to identify. The five climbers had to think like detectives. They examined the body and its clothes. The nametag on the old cotton shirt read "G Mallory"!

---

develop: to create a picture from film
decayed: broken-down; rotten
identify: to show or prove to be a certain person or thing
detective: a person who gathers information to solve a problem or crime
examine: to look at closely

Mallory (second from left) and company, 1922

Where Is the Camera?

They had found Mallory's body. But there was no sign of the camera.

The climbers buried Mallory under rocks and said a prayer. Still today, his remains lie on the mountain where he fell. Irvine's body has not yet been found.

---

remains: a dead body

Route to the Summit

There is more than one route to Everest's summit. A climber can scale the north side or the south side. Mallory and Irvine had chosen the north, the hardest route. This climb includes a 100-foot (30.5-meter) rock wall called the "Second Step." Mallory and Irvine were supposed to climb it on the way to the summit.

View of Mt. Everest from the north

Lead climber, Conrad Anker

Climbing the Second Step

Conrad Anker, the U.S. search team's lead climber, prepared to scale the Second Step. If he made it, that would show that Mallory and Irvine could have done it, too. Then it's possible they could have reached the summit first.

Anker started early in the morning. He did not use any ropes. The climb took a few minutes. He said it was hard, but Mallory and Irvine could have done it.

But had they? And had they finally reached the summit? Only Mount Everest knows for sure!

Mallory and Irvine tried to climb a great mountain. Polo searched for a great empire. We may never know whether any of them succeeded. In Chapter 3, meet a sailor who tried to sail around the world— and made it!

Return of the *Golden Hinde*

The Golden Hinde *was one of England's most famous warships. It was also one of the first ships to sail around the world. A copy of the* Golden Hinde *can be seen in London today. But what happened to the real thing?*

Sir Francis Drake

Sir Francis Drake

England has a proud maritime past. It has been home to many famous sailors. Its shipyards have built many great ships.

Sir Francis Drake is one of history's most famous sailors. From 1577 to 1580, he sailed around the world. He was the first Englishman to make this amazing journey.

During the voyage, Drake raided Spanish ports on the Pacific coast of Peru and Mexico. His ship returned to London loaded with stolen gold and silver. Still, everyone in England praised Drake and his crew as heroes. Queen Elizabeth I even made him a knight.

Of course, every sailor needs a ship! Drake had a good one, the *Golden Hinde*.

---

maritime: having to do with sailing or shipping on the sea
voyage: a journey by water
raid: to attack suddenly
knight: a man given high social rank and allowed to use *Sir* before his name

The *Golden Hinde*

Drake began his voyage with five ships.
The *Golden Hinde* was his flagship. This
galleon had five decks, including a gun
deck with 22 cannons. Only the *Golden
Hinde* completed the journey around
the world.

A carving from the Golden Hinde

---

flagship: the main ship of a fleet where the commander is
galleon: a large sailing ship with three masts

Left to Rot

At the end of her journey, the *Golden Hinde* sailed up the Thames River. She arrived in London, wrapped in giant banners. The great ship's sailing days were over. She remained tied up at Deptford Docks for more than 100 years.

Over time, the *Golden Hinde* began to fall apart. Her rotting timbers could not be repaired. No one knew how to save her. Finally, this reminder of Drake's epic voyage was lost.

Keeping History Alive

But the story of the *Golden Hinde* does not end with a rotten ship. In 1971, nearly 400 years after she first sailed, English craftsmen started to build a copy of the ship. They wanted a replica to celebrate her great journey. They wanted to keep history alive!

---

timber: wood used for building
replica: an exact copy

Starting from Scratch

Building a new *Golden Hinde* was a huge task. Any records or plans of the old ship had been lost. How would the craftsmen know what to build?

A naval architect named Christian Norgaard (NOHR-gard) designed a new ship. To do this, he researched the history of the *Golden Hinde*. He read old books and studied paintings of the ship. He even read the diary of the ship's chaplain, Francis Fletcher.

The replica was built at Hinks Shipyard, in Devon, England. The new *Golden Hinde* took almost two years to build. She looked just like Drake's famous ship. Her crew even dressed as 16th-century sailors!

---

craftsman: a person with special skill in making things
naval architect: a person who designs ships
research: to study facts
chaplain: a minister, priest, or rabbi serving in the armed forces

Aboard the new Golden Hinde, *everyone wears 16th-century clothing.*

25

Around the World Again!

The new *Golden Hinde* was launched on April 5, 1973. In 1974, she sailed west across the Atlantic Ocean toward the United States. This was the same route Sir Francis Drake had taken nearly 400 years before.

launch: to cause to slide into the water and set afloat

For the next six years, the new *Golden Hinde* sailed all the way around the world. She visited more than 300 ports. Huge crowds came to see her.

The *Golden Hinde* returned to London in 1980. That year marked the 400th birthday of Drake's epic voyage.

The new Golden Hinde

The new Golden Hinde *sets sail.*

History Lesson

Today, the new *Golden Hinde* is docked in London. Thousands of adults and children tour it every year. They walk the gangplank and go below decks. They see what life was like for a sailor in the 16th century. The new *Golden Hinde* keeps Drake's voyage alive!

Drake's voyage around the world made him a great explorer. More than 220 years later, two other great explorers headed out on their own journey. It was a journey across America. Who were they? What do you think they saw?

gangplank: a ramp that moves and is used for entering or leaving a ship

— CHAPTER **4** —

Exploring America

It is 1803. A new nation is growing. Americans have wild lands to explore, full of unknown dangers. Imagine being one of the explorers to set out across this strange, new land. Do you think you would be brave enough?

Lewis and Clark (right) with Sacagawea

A New Nation

In 1803, the United States was a young nation with a new government. Its citizens had thousands of miles of wild land they knew nothing about.

President Thomas Jefferson called for an expedition to explore this land. The United States' finest young soldiers would explore from the Missouri River to the Pacific Ocean. Captain Meriwether Lewis and Lieutenant William Clark were chosen to lead the group, called the Corps of Discovery.

On May 21, 1804, the Corps set off down the Missouri River. Questions filled their heads. Was there a water route all the way to the Pacific? What sort of animals lived in these lands? Were the Indians friendly or hostile?

---

hostile: like an enemy; warlike

To the Pacific

The journey lasted two and a half years. Lewis and Clark's team followed the Missouri River and then crossed the Rocky Mountains. They went all the way to the Pacific Ocean!

They wrote about everything they saw. They were treated well by the Indian tribes they met. The land was beautiful and filled with wildlife the soldiers had never before seen. Lewis and Clark's team drew maps of their travel. Now others could follow in their steps.

Map of Lewis and Clark's Expedition

Time to Celebrate

Others did follow, and the land became more and more settled. Now, 200 years later, the United States plans to celebrate Lewis and Clark's journey. President George W. Bush has said that 2003–2006 will be the Lewis and Clark Bicentennial.

President Bush called the Lewis and Clark expedition "an epic of endurance and discovery." He said, "it changed the face of our country forever ... all Americans should know about (it), and they should teach their children about it, as well."

Lewis and Clark Monument, Great Falls, Montana

---

bicentennial: happening once every 200 years
endurance: the ability to hold up or survive hardship

Honoring the Brave

The Bicentennial will not just honor the memories of Lewis and Clark. It will also honor the spirit and courage of the Corps of Discovery. Hundreds of anniversary events will take place.

For one event, craftsmen in St. Charles, Missouri, have built a replica of the boat that Lewis and Clark used. It is called a *keelboat* and is 55 feet (16.8 meters) long and weighs 7 tons (6,350 kilograms). This keelboat took two years to build. The oarsmen will dress in clothes from the 19th century. They are planning to reenact the first expedition.

---

anniversary: celebrating something that happened on a certain date
keelboat: a large, shallow boat with a center plate running along the bottom of the ship
oarsman: a person who rows
reenact: to perform again an event that happened before

The replica of the Lewis and Clark keelboat

Lewis and Clark showed courage as they headed west across uncharted land. A little more than 100 years later, another brave explorer set out. Her trail was one Lewis and Clark probably never dreamed of. It was through the air.

---

uncharted: not marked on a map; not explored or known

— CHAPTER **5** —

Amelia Earhart

In 1937, Amelia Earhart tried to fly farther than any woman had before. She tried to fly around the world! Sadly, she died trying. Sixty years later, someone would try to finish what Earhart started.

Amelia Earhart

Crossing the Atlantic

Amelia Earhart (uh-MEEL-yah AIR-hart) was 10 years old when she saw her first airplane. "It was a thing of rusty wire and wood and not at all interesting," she said later. But Earhart's ideas about airplanes would soon change.

In the early 1900s, airplanes were still very new. A female pilot was rarer still. Earhart rode in a plane for the first time at age 23 in 1920. She was hooked! Soon she started taking flying lessons.

In 1928, Earhart was asked to join an attempt to fly across the Atlantic Ocean. She would be the first woman to cross the Atlantic by plane.

From June 17 to June 18, 1928, Earhart and two other pilots, Wilmer Stultz and Louis Gordon, flew across the Atlantic. Earhart had earned her place in the record books. But she wanted to do more. She wanted to fly around the world!

---

rare: not common

Lost without a Trace

On June 1, 1937, Earhart and her navigator, Fred Noonan, began Earhart's dream flight. If successful, Earhart would be the first woman to fly around the world. She would also travel the longest possible route. She would go around the globe at its middle. Earhart and Noonan crossed Africa and Asia. They only stopped to refuel and check the plane.

By June 29, they had covered 22,000 miles (35,405 kilometers). But the Pacific Ocean was still ahead of them.

Over the Pacific, Earhart's plane disappeared. No one knows why. Maybe it ran out of fuel. Maybe it broke down. The plane and its crew were never found.

America mourned the loss of one of its boldest pilots. But Earhart's legend would continue to grow.

---

navigator: a person who plans and controls the course of a ship or plane
mourn: to be sad over someone's death
legend: a story passed down

Honoring Earhart

Earhart never flew around the world. Today, thousands of people have done it. But Earhart's brave journey is still remembered.

Sixty years later, in 1997, another pilot decided to honor Earhart in a special way. Linda Finch was a 46-year-old mom from Texas. For Earhart's 100th birthday, Finch decided to repeat Earhart's flight around the world!

Finch wanted to follow the same route as Earhart. She even planned to use a similar plane. But she would change one thing. Finch would use modern navigation and communication methods. She needed to, because she planned to fly alone!

---

navigation: the act or skill of steering a course

Only 28,500 Miles to Go

Finch set off from Oakland, California, on March 17, 1997. Ahead of her was a journey of 28,500 miles (45,866 kilometers). Would she make it?

Finch flew at a height of 6,000 to 8,000 feet (1,829 to 2,438 meters). Modern planes fly much higher.

Finch followed Earhart's flight plan almost exactly. She even flew over the place where Earhart most likely crashed. Finch dropped three wreaths there to honor Earhart's memory.

Finch landed back in Oakland on May 28. She had been to five continents. She had made 34 stops in 18 countries. Remember Sir Francis Drake and the *Golden Hinde?* It had taken Drake nearly three years to sail around the world. Finch had flown around the world in 72 days! "It was a very delightful flight," she said. "The airplane was great."

---

wreath: a ring of leaves and flowers twisted together
delightful: pleasing

Linda Finch arrives in Oakland on May 28, 1997, after her flight around the world.

Celebrating the Spirit of Adventure

All these amazing journeys share something. They celebrate the spirit of adventure. People have always explored the world they live in. They have tested their limits of courage and endurance. As long as there are amazing journeys to make, new explorers will set out to make them. Are there any amazing journeys in your future?

Epilogue

Flight to Australia

In 1919, brothers Ross and Keith Smith flew from England to Australia. They were the first to fly the 11,000-mile (17,702-kilometer) trip. They showed the world that it was possible to fly long distances.

In 1994, Peter McMillan and Lang Kidby flew the same journey in a rebuilt Vimy, the plane the Smiths had used. Find out more on www.vimy.org.

First to the North Pole

In 1909, the U.S. explorers Robert Peary and Matthew Henson became the first men to reach the North Pole. Their success was a huge team effort. Their helpers included 130 huskies pulling sleds of supplies.

In 1990, Børge Ousland and Erling Kagge, from Norway, also reached the North Pole. They were the first to do so without getting supplies from the outside. Check out www.northpole1909.com.

The *Mayflower* Sails Again

In 1620, a group of English people sailed from Plymouth, England to North America. These people were later called *Pilgrims*. In the 1950s, a replica of one of the ships they traveled on, the *Mayflower*, was built in England. In April 1957, this replica sailed the same journey made famous by the Pilgrims.

The *Mayflower II*, as she is known, is now docked at Plimoth Plantation, Massachusetts. See www.plimoth.org/Museum/Mayflower/mayflowe.htm.

Workers build a replica of the Mayflower *in this 1956 photograph.*

Glossary

anniversary: celebrating something that happened on a certain date

bicentennial: happening once every 200 years

chaplain: a minister, priest, or rabbi serving in the armed forces

chopsticks: a pair of small sticks held in one hand and used to lift food to the mouth

craftsman: a person with special skill in making things

decayed: broken-down; rotten

delightful: pleasing

detective: a person who gathers information to solve a problem or crime

develop: to create a picture from film

dictate: to speak aloud while another writes what you say

endurance: the ability to hold up or survive hardship

epic: a type of poem or story about the adventures of great heroes

European: a person born or living in Europe

examine: to look at closely

expedition: a group making a long trip for a special purpose

flagship: the main ship of a fleet where the commander is

flourish: to be successful and prosper

galleon: a large sailing ship with three masts

gangplank: a ramp that moves and is used for entering or leaving a ship

honor: to show great respect

hostile: like an enemy; warlike

identify: to show or prove to be a certain person or thing

keelboat: a large, shallow boat with a center plate running along the bottom of the ship

knight: a man given high social rank and allowed to use *Sir* before his name

launch: to cause to slide into the water and set afloat

legend: a story passed down

maritime: having to do with sailing or shipping on the sea

merchant: a person who sells goods

mourn: to be sad over someone's death

naval architect: a person who designs ships

navigation: the act or skill of steering a course

navigator: a person who plans and controls the course of a ship or plane

oarsman: a person who rows

oxygen: a gas that all plants and animals need to live

raid: to attack suddenly

rare: not common

reenact: to perform again an event that happened before

remains: a dead body

replica: an exact copy

research: to study facts

satellite: an object put into orbit around a planet or moon

scale: to climb up something; to reach the highest point of

summit: the highest point

timber: wood used for building

trek: a long, slow journey

uncharted: not marked on a map; not explored or known

vehicle: a means of carrying people or things over land

voyage: a journey by water

wreath: a ring of leaves and flowers twisted together

Bibliography

Bledsoe, Glen and Karen. *Ballooning Adventures.* Dangerous Adventures. Mankato, Minn.: Capstone Press, 2001.

Bull, Angela. *Flying Ace: The Story of Amelia Earhart.* Eyewitness Readers. New York: DK Publishing, 2000.

Dowswell, Paul. *True Everest Adventure Stories.* Usborne True Stories. London: Usborne Publishing Ltd, 2002.

Johmann, Carol A. *The Lewis & Clark Expedition: Join the Corps of Discovery to Explore Uncharted Territory.* Charlotte, Va.: Williamson Publishing, 2002.

McLoone, Margo. *Women Explorers in Africa: Christina Dodwell, Delia Akeley, Mary Kingsley, Florence von Sass-Baker, Alexandrine Tinne.* Capstone Short Biographies. Mankato, Minn.: Capstone Press, 1997.

Useful Addresses

The *Golden Hinde*
St Mary Overie Dock, Cathedral Street, London
SE1 9DE
United Kingdom

Lewis and Clark Trail Heritage Foundation
P.O. Box 3434
Great Falls, MT 59403

The Quest Channel
8000 Marina Blvd., Suite 400
Brisbane, CA 94005

Internet Sites

Amelia Earhart
http://www.ameliaearhart.com

Everest
http://www.pbs.org/wgbh/nova/everest

Lewis and Clark Trail Heritage Foundation, Inc.
http://www.lewisandclark.org

The Quest Channel
http://www.quest.classroom.com

Sir Francis Drake
http://www.sirfrancisdrakehistory.net

Index